WHY I Believe in Jesus
(and Why You Should, too)

Peter C. Hamilton

Lynchburg, VA
www.liberty.edu/libertyuniversitypress

Why I Believe in Jesus (and Why You Should, Too),
Copyright © Peter C. Hamilton, 2013

All Rights Reserved. Except as permitted under the U.S. Copyright Act of 1976, no part of this publication may be reproduced by any means, electronic or mechanical, including photocopying, recording, or by any information storage retrieval system, without permission of the copyright's owner, except for the inclusion of brief quotations for a review.

Liberty University Press
1971 University Blvd.
Lynchburg, VA 24502

www.liberty.edu/libertyuniversitypress

Scripture taken from the *New King James Version®*. Copyright © 1982 by Thomas Nelson, Inc. Used by permission. All rights reserved.

ISBN: 978-1-935986-50-8

First ebook edition, June 2013
First trade paperback edition, June 2013

10 9 8 7 6 5 4 3 2 1

Printed in the United States of America

Book Design by Coreen Montagna

Table of Contents

Introduction..I
Do You Believe in Jesus Christ?..3
Reasons to Believe in Jesus...5
Reason #1..7
Reason #2..9
Reason #3..11
Reason #4..13
Other Reasons to Believe..17
He Changed My Life — My Personal Testimony............19
So What Does it Mean to Believe in Jesus......................23
Invitation to Believe in Jesus Christ...............................27
God's Plan of Salvation...29
A Prayer to Receive Jesus...31
About the Author..33

To Joyce, my wife for thirty-one wonderful years, and to our children, Rebecca and John.

Introduction

This book is written to encourage you to believe in Jesus and to answer basic questions that people often have concerning what it means to be a believer. This book also provides solid reasons for believing in Jesus based on the teachings of the Bible.

First, why should a person believe in Jesus? What, if anything, makes Him different or unique among the leaders of world religions? Is He just one among many saviors, or is He the only Savior, as many of His followers claim?

Second, what does it mean to believe in Jesus? A lot of people say they believe in Him. For many, believing in Jesus simply means accepting what has been written in the Bible concerning Him. These accounts describe His activities two thousand years ago in Palestine which are associated with the start of Christianity. Certain things about the life of Jesus, such as His gathering of disciples, His ministry of teaching, His healing miracles, and His death by crucifixion are usually included in this basic belief system.

People with a basic belief in Jesus may also believe on a more personal level that He died for their sins, but they may not claim to have a personal relationship with Him or say that He makes a difference in their daily lives. For others, believing in Jesus means they have committed every aspect of their lives to Him, and they say that He has changed their lives dramatically.

The distinction between these types of believers might be described as the difference between an intellectual belief of the head and a saving faith of the heart. It is the difference between a stagnant, emotionally neutral belief that has little impact on a person's life and a vibrant, heartfelt one that affects every area of daily life.

Which kind of believer are you? If you are not yet a believer, which kind do you think you would choose to be?

Do You Believe in Jesus?

When I refer to believing in Jesus, I am not just indicating the acceptance of historical accounts in the Bible. Saving faith certainly includes believing what the Bible says about Him, but there is more to it than that. For one thing, it involves repentance from sin. You may wonder, "What is sin? And what does it mean to repent?" The Bible defines sin in a number of ways, but the essence of sin is living for self rather than living for God. Repentance means forsaking an attitude of independence from God and coming to a new understanding of man's primary reason for living. It entails making a conscious decision to follow Jesus.

Jesus explains what it means to follow Him. First, He states the primary act is self-denial. *Then Jesus said to His disciples, "If anyone desires to come after Me, let him deny himself, and take up his cross, and follow Me"* (Matthew 16:24). So the decision to follow Him involves moving from a self-centered lifestyle to a Christ-centered one. That transformation is the essence of repentance. Another important aspect of following Jesus is relying on His power rather than your own. This change involves telling God that you are tired of doing things your way and ready to do things His way. You tell Jesus that you want to yield control of your life to Him and that you are ready to commit your life to Him.

When I ask if you believe in Jesus, I am asking if you have come to the place of trusting in Him as your only hope of eternal salvation rather than believing that your own goodness and efforts are sufficient. Is that your understanding of what it means to believe in Jesus?

Reasons to Believe in Jesus

If you are already a believer, the next question is, "Why do you believe in Jesus?" Suppose somebody came up to you and asked that question. How would you answer?

The Bible presents many reasons to believe in Jesus. I will share some of the main reasons that I believe in Him. The following passage from 1 Corinthians contains a basic outline of the Gospel message presented in the New Testament. *Moreover, brethren, I declare to you the gospel which I preached to you, which also you received and in which you stand, by which also you are saved, if you hold fast that word which I preached to you — unless you believed in vain. For I delivered to you first of all that which I also received: that Christ died for our sins according to the Scriptures, and that He was buried, and that He rose again the third day according to the Scriptures, and that He was seen by Cephas, then by the twelve. After that He was seen by over five hundred brethren at once, of whom the greater part remain to the present, but some have fallen asleep. After that He was seen by James, then by all the apostles* (1 Corinthians 15:1-7).

The Christian Gospel is the *good news* that Jesus died for your sins, that He has risen from the dead, and that all who believe in Him will be eternally saved. As a result, we can have our sins forgiven and go to Heaven when we die. The writers of the New Testament all agree that eternal salvation can only occur if we put our faith in Jesus. Jesus told His own disciples that He is the only way to God. He said to them, *"I am the way, the truth, and the life. No one comes to the Father except through Me"* (John 14:6). There are several reasons that Jesus is able to make that claim which provide further grounds for believing in Him.

Reason #1:
The Virgin Birth of Jesus

I believe in Jesus because He has existed eternally as God and entered human history as Jesus of Nazareth through the miracle of the virgin birth. The Christian doctrine of the virgin birth reveals that Jesus was no ordinary man, but God in human flesh, *the God-man*. Jesus is fully divine as well as fully human. Even though He created everything that exists and everything was created for His glory, He came into the world as the promised Messiah expected by Israel for centuries. He came to fulfill God's plan of salvation for all who are willing to put their trust in Him.

Christians celebrate this miraculous birth during the Christmas season. The Bible states that Jesus, the eternal Word, became flesh and dwelt among us (John 1:14). He showed us what God is like, and He also showed us how we should live as humans, by voluntarily humbling Himself so that He could walk among us. He temporarily laid aside some of the privileges of deity so that He could become our Savior.

I believe in Jesus because He is the God-man who entered human history through the miracle of the virgin birth.

Reason #2:
The Sinless Life of Jesus

I believe in Jesus because, according to the Scriptures, He lived a sinless life. The word of God, which is the divinely inspired record of eyewitnesses who knew Jesus personally, states that Jesus *"...was in all points tempted as we are, yet without sin"* (Hebrews 4:15). He never committed a single sin. If He had not lived a sinless life, He could not be our Savior.

This is one reason the doctrine of the virgin birth of Jesus is important. It tells us that He was not born with a sinful nature like us. All other humans have a mother and father who passed their fallen nature on to us at birth. Jesus had a human mother, Mary, but His father is God. As a result, Jesus did not inherit the sinful nature of all other descendants of Adam. The Bible also tells us that He faced temptation on many occasions during His earthly ministry, but He refused to give in to a single temptation even when facing death on the cross. Consequently, He was able to offer Himself up as the perfect sacrifice for sin.

John the Baptist called Him, *"The Lamb of God who takes away the sin of the world!"* (John 1:29). The Scriptures of the Old Testament provide the background for understanding the importance of an unblemished sacrifice to atone for sin.

In ancient Israel, lambs and other animals were sacrificed on a regular basis. There were two daily sacrifices, one in the morning and one in the evening. There were special sacrifices for different occasions to meet specific needs in the lives of God's people. Every sacrificial animal had to be free of disease or defect.

There were yearly sacrifices for the people. In the institution of the Jewish festival called Passover, a lamb without blemish was sacrificed to provide protection from death for Israel's firstborn. Also, there was a special sacrifice on the Day of Atonement that provided forgiveness for the sins of all of God's people. Once a year, on that special day, the high priest went into a sacred tent to sprinkle the blood of the sacrifice in the presence of God. As a result, God forgave the sins of His people. Just like the unblemished lambs in the ancient sacrificial rites, Jesus had to be without sin in order to be a sacrifice for the sins of this world.

When Jesus died for our sins on the cross, He provided a way for all who put their trust in Him to be forgiven and to be delivered from eternal death, which is separation from God in a place called Hell. Jesus is the Lamb of God who took away the sins of the world by bearing our sins in His own body on the cross.

I believe in Jesus because He is the God-man who entered human history through the miracle of the virgin birth. I believe in Jesus because He lived a sinless life.

Reason #3:
The Sacrificial Death of Jesus

I believe in Jesus because He took the judgment we deserve for our sins when He died on the cross. Simply stated, He died for our sins (1 Corinthians 15:3). The death of Jesus was no accident. Jesus told His disciples that He would, as an act of His own free will, lay down His life. No one could take it from Him by force. Men who were unwilling to believe in Him were involved in condemning Him to death and carrying out His execution, but Jesus was not merely the victim of some cruel plot of sinful men. His death on the cross has always been the sovereign plan of God.

The Book of Revelation reveals that Jesus is *"...the Lamb slain from the foundation of the world"* (Revelation 13:8). God the Father, God the Son (Jesus), and God the Holy Spirit decided together in Heaven before the dawn of human history that Jesus' willing sacrifice would make our redemption possible. Before any human being lived on Earth, it was God's plan to provide a way of salvation.

There is a purpose in the death of Jesus that goes way beyond the religious or political circumstances of first century Palestine. Hebrews 9:22 says, *"...without shedding of blood there is no remission."* The word remission means forgiveness, so the verse means without the shedding of blood, there is no forgiveness of sin. It is only through the death of Jesus Christ on the cross that the proper payment for our sins could be made. We receive that gift by putting our trust in Him.

The New Testament makes it clear that He died for the sins of the entire human race—for everyone who has ever lived or who will live on this planet. John 3:16 says, *"For God so loved the world that He gave His only begotten Son, that whoever believes in Him should not perish but have everlasting life."* In this verse, "the world" refers to all people. The phrase, "whoever believes in Him" means whoever trusts in Him. This verse makes it clear that we need to believe in Jesus if we want to have everlasting life in Heaven. Simply believing a few facts about who Jesus is or what He did will not save anyone. We must trust in Him as our only hope of eternal salvation if we want to go to Heaven. We will come back to this important truth later.

Jesus was born of a virgin. Jesus lived a sinless life. Jesus offered up His life on the cross so that you and I could be forgiven of our sins. All we have to do is place our faith in Him. What an amazing God! What an incredible plan of salvation!

I believe in Jesus because He was born of a virgin. I believe in Jesus because He lived a sinless life. I believe in Jesus because He died for my sins, for your sins, and for the sins of the entire world.

Reason #4:
The Resurrection of Jesus from the Dead

I believe in Jesus because He rose from the dead. Following His crucifixion, He came back to life and appeared to His disciples multiple times over a period of several weeks. These post-resurrection appearances provide convincing proof that He is exactly who He says He is. Jesus is the eternal Son of God, the Lamb slain from the foundation of the world. He died on the cross and rose again, so those who trust in Him could live forever in eternal glory.

Before He went to the cross, Jesus warned His disciples more than once that it was going to happen. He told them that He would be crucified, that He would be in the grave for three days, and that on the third day He would rise again. The disciples believed Jesus to be the Messiah, but when He died on the cross, they thought His ministry had come to a tragic and premature end. They had a difficult time comprehending His warnings. They had seen Him raise other people from the dead, but when He was crucified, they lacked both faith and understanding that he could come back from the grave. It was not until the Sunday morning when He came out of the tomb that they finally began to understand what He had been trying to tell them.

Immediately following the crucifixion of Christ, biblical accounts depict a group of Christ-followers who were huddled together feeling discouraged, dreading discovery by the authorities who crucified Jesus, and fearing for their own lives. Jesus first appeared to some of the women who were His followers and then to many of His disciples on multiple occasions. Some of them had already gone back to doing what they were doing when they first met Him. Peter, James, and John are examples. Disappointed and discouraged, they went back to their fishing nets. Then, Jesus came and met with them. He appeared to them several times and in several different places to prove that He is alive. The Gospel accounts in Matthew, Mark, Luke, and John describe several post-resurrection appearances of Jesus. According to 1 Corinthians 15:6, He appeared to more than five hundred of His disciples at one time before He ascended back to Heaven.

If you read the rest of 1 Corinthians 15, it becomes clear that if Jesus had not been raised from the dead, Christianity would be a waste of time. It would do us absolutely no good to believe in Him if He were still in the grave. If this were the case, we might as well stop reading our Bibles, stop going to church, and stop trying to encourage other people to believe in Him. Without the resurrection of Jesus, we are still in our sins.

The truth is, however, that Jesus did come back from the dead! The New Testament books are eyewitness accounts of Jesus' life, death, and resurrection. He was seen alive by His disciples on many different occasions following the resurrection, which means we can also believe in Him as they did. If Jesus had not been raised from the dead and had not appeared to His disciples afterwards, do you think they would have been willing to give up their lives for Him? Do you think that if they were put on a witness stand under the threat of death and asked what really happened, that their stories would all match? Don't you think at least one of them would have considered his own self-preservation more important than going to his death if it had all been a lie? Jesus' first followers saw Him alive following His crucifixion! Many of them suffered for their faith and some even died proclaiming his resurrection. Based on their testimony recorded in Scripture, we can have confidence that this is all true.

After the resurrection, the disciples understood all that Jesus had done in order to save them from their sins and they trusted in Him wholeheartedly from that time forward. They finally understood the purpose of Jesus' death and resurrection. They understood that it was necessary for Him to die on the cross for their sins and for the sins of the entire world. They also understood that He is victorious over death, so He could give those who believe in Him victory over death as well. Jesus has made it possible for those who believe in Him to live forever with Him in Heaven.

Think about it. If Jesus did not rise from the dead as His disciples say He did, there is no point for Christians to worship or study what the Scriptures say. But if He truly is the risen Savior, we have every reason to worship and serve Him! If Jesus truly is the God-man who was born of a virgin, if He truly lived a sinless life, if He truly died on the cross for your sins and for mine, and if He truly has risen from the dead, then why wouldn't we believe in Him?

Other Reasons to Believe in Jesus

There are other reasons for choosing to believe in Him. First, Old Testament prophecy was fulfilled at Jesus' birth and at other times during His life and ministry. Prophecies written hundreds of years before He walked upon Earth were fulfilled in amazing detail. They serve as further evidence that Jesus is who He says He is.

Another reason to believe in Jesus is His promised return. He told His disciples that He will come again to set up His kingdom here on Earth. He will come back for His own people. Jesus promises that when He sets up His kingdom here on Earth, His followers will rule with Him.

He Changed My Life

Ultimately though, one of the biggest reasons I believe in Jesus and have decided to follow Him is because He changed my life and continues to work in it daily. This change began when I made the decision to receive Him as my personal Savior and Lord.

A religious leader named Nicodemus once came to Jesus to talk to Him about what it means to be a true follower of God. Jesus said to him, *"...unless one is born again, he cannot see the kingdom of God"* (John 3:3). He explained to Nicodemus that even though he was a religious man and a student of the Scriptures, there was one thing he lacked. He needed to be born spiritually through the work of the Holy Spirit. He needed to repent of his sins and place his faith in the Lord Jesus Christ. I needed to do the same thing. Like Nicodemus, I was lost in sin and in need of repentance.

I have attended church for as long as I can remember. I thought of myself as a Christian and a good person and I hoped that I would go to Heaven one day. I was basing that hope on my church membership, moral values, and good deeds. However, because my hope was based on my own personal works, I was not certain that I would be able to go to Heaven.

Then a friend of mine began to share with me that I could know Jesus personally. He told me I could know for sure that my sins were forgiven and that I was on my way to Heaven. He told me I could have a personal relationship with God that would make a difference in my daily life.

I was skeptical at first and even a little offended. I had gone to church all my life. I told him I had my own form of religion, so I did not need him to tell me what it meant to be a Christian. Nevertheless, over the course of a few months, I began to notice some things had changed in his life for the better. I came to realize that I needed that kind of change in my own life.

As hard as I tried, I found that I was completely unable to change my own behavior in any meaningful way. As a person who was blessed with a good family and many material comforts, I should have been happy. Instead, I was sad and depressed about circumstances that I could not change. With all of the good things that had been given to me, I should have been thankful. Instead, I found myself getting angry at other people for letting me down in small ways or for not responding to me in a manner that I thought they should. I actually thought of myself as a loser at one point in my life and I had developed a rather negative outlook for the future.

I now know that the only change that really matters is the change that God makes in my life. He has done so many things that I could not have accomplished by myself. Another major difference between religion and biblical Christianity is demonstrated through my testimony. God changed me when I decided to believe in Jesus and He is still changing me as I walk with Him each day. Salvation is by the grace of God alone, through faith alone, and in Jesus alone. It is not about what I can do for God. It is about what God has done for me and continues to do in me through Christ.

I attended church as far back as I can remember, but I did not know Jesus as my personal Savior until

I was nineteen years old. After my friend showed me what God was doing in his life and shared God's plan for salvation, I finally understood that believing was as simple as inviting Jesus into my life. I decided to ask Him to forgive me of my sins and to be my personal Savior. I am so glad I did! He changed my life forever.

So What Does It Mean to Believe in Jesus?

This question brings up an interesting thought concerning the word "believe." I have often wondered why some people say they believe in Jesus but do not allow Him to influence their daily lives. Is it possible to believe in Jesus intellectually without really believing in Him the way the Bible says we should? Is it possible to believe what the Bible says about Jesus and what He did for us on the cross, and even claim to be one of His followers, but not actually know Him? Is there a difference between being religious and having a relationship with Him?

If you talk to people about what it means to "believe" in Jesus, you will get various answers. People sometimes talk about "getting religion," almost making it sound like a disease. I tried being religious, but my religion only insulated me from a relationship with Jesus. Another thing people sometimes talk about when saying they "believe" is changing their lives for the better. What I want to ask them is, did YOU change your life, or did GOD change your life? There is a big difference between those two things. I have found that I can change very little about myself without God's help.

I once heard someone say that the distinction between knowing about Jesus and truly knowing Jesus is only eighteen inches, the distance between your head and your heart. To readdress my previous point, there is a big difference between intellectual belief of the head and saving faith of the heart.

Many people believe in Jesus the same way they believe in George Washington or another historical figure. For instance, they believe that George Washington led the Colonial Army during the American Revolution, held the army together during that horrible winter at Valley Forge, and became the first president of the United States. Similarly, some people believe a few historical facts about Jesus, such as He lived in Palestine around two thousand years ago, gathered some followers, healed sick people, was crucified, and so on. Their belief does not go beyond acceptance of those historical facts. Both Washington and Jesus are historical figures, but I have never heard anyone say they are expecting George Washington to do anything for them now or in the future. Jesus is much more than a historical figure. He is the living Savior! Intellectual belief in Jesus goes as far as accepting the historical record of His life and ministry as it is revealed in the Bible. Saving faith, however, goes beyond that head knowledge to a personal trust in Him that includes a life commitment.

John 3:16 says, *"For God so loved the world that He gave His only begotten Son, that whoever believes in Him should not perish but have everlasting life."* If believing in Jesus is how we avoid perishing in Hell and how we enter eternal bliss in Heaven, it is essential that we understand what it means to believe in Him. So how do we "believe" in Him?

The Bible says that eternal salvation is possible because God in the person of Jesus Christ stepped out of Heaven to take our place on the cross. He took the punishment that we deserve for the sins we have committed. Jesus was willing to give up His rightful place in Heaven and all the privileges of being the Son of God to come to this sinful world where he was mistreated and eventually killed by sinners. He did it so that we might have an intimate relationship with Him.

Ephesians 2:8-9 puts it this way: *"For by grace you have been saved through faith, and that not of yourselves; it is the gift of God, not of works, lest anyone should boast."* When I first read and understood these verses, it was like a light switched on inside my brain. I used to think that I was responsible for getting myself to Heaven. I thought salvation was the result of going to church and being a good person. These verses say something very different. Salvation must be received as a gift from God! I cannot earn it, nor can I do anything to deserve it. If I could, I would be boasting about what I had done to get to Heaven, like all the others who worked their way there. But that would not be Heaven, would it? It would be no different than Earth, where people boast about their achievements and try to outdo each other.

Until you allow Jesus to come into your life, open your eyes to the truth of His Word, and ask Him to become your Savior, the message of the Bible will remain a mystery to you. I have known quite a few people who say they have read the Bible but did not get much out of it. This may be because they do not know the Author because they have never been introduced to Him personally.

When I received Christ as my personal Lord and Savior, I learned the difference between man-made religion and a God-created relationship. Religion is man's attempt to reach God through personal effort and good works. Most religions of the world (and even some varieties of Christianity) teach that you must earn or work your way into Heaven. The Bible teaches that salvation cannot be achieved or earned by human effort. It must be received as a gift from God. "Believing" in Jesus and receiving the gift of salvation is something that occurs when you open your heart to Him, make the decision to believe His Word, and accept his free gift of eternal life. I will never forget the day that I decided to put my trust in Jesus. I will never stop thanking God for the things He has done in my life.

An Invitation to Believe in Jesus

Do you believe in Jesus? If you do, does your belief in Him impact your daily life? If you do not yet believe in Jesus the way that I have described, would you like to take that step of faith?

Believing in Jesus is really quite simple, but it can also be rather costly. Jesus once told His disciples that they should count the cost of following Him before beginning that journey. The kind of belief in Jesus that is life-changing is not the most popular thing in our modern society. You may lose a friend or two. You may even make an enemy or two along the way depending on how serious you are about following Jesus.

Jesus sums up the cost by saying, *"...whoever of you does not forsake all that he has cannot be My disciple"* (Luke 14:33). Does this verse mean that you have to get rid of all your possessions and live the life of a monk? Not necessarily. It does mean that you cannot allow your possessions or the desire to accumulate more to get in the way of following Jesus. At the heart of His statement is a challenge to pursue the most important things in life. I am referring to things that are eternal rather than temporal, things that are spiritual rather than material.

Jesus once spoke of the "true riches" (Luke 16:11). These are riches or rewards that are given to the individual who lives for Him rather than for worldly wealth or selfish ambition.

Believing in Jesus begins with receiving Him. John 1:12 says, *"But as many as received Him, to them He gave the right to become children of God, to those who believe in His name."* Receiving Jesus is the first step toward believing in Him as a way of life. Receiving Jesus is a conscious decision to invite Him into your life and to start living for Him rather than for yourself. The following Bible verses provide a basic outline of the Gospel message and explain what it means to believe in Jesus.

God's Plan of Salvation

1. We have all sinned. In other words, no one is perfect. *"...for all have sinned and fall short of the glory of God."* (Romans 3:23)

2. You can put your trust in the Savior who died for your sins and rose again. *"For I delivered to you first of all that which I also received: that Christ died for our sins according to the Scriptures, and that He was buried, and that He rose again the third day according to the Scriptures."* (1 Corinthians 15:3-4)

3. You must face death because of your sin, but you can receive God's gift of eternal life. *"For the wages of sin is death, but the gift of God is eternal life in Christ Jesus our Lord."* (Romans 6:23)

4. You cannot save yourself through good works. *"For by grace you have been saved through faith, and that not of yourselves; it is the gift of God, not of works, lest anyone should boast."* (Ephesians 2:8-9)

5. You need to stop living for yourself and start living for Jesus. *"Repent therefore and be converted, that your sins may be blotted out, so that times of refreshing may come from the presence of the Lord..."* (Acts 3:19)

6. You receive Christ by personal invitation. *"For 'whoever calls on the name of the Lord shall be saved.'"* (Romans 10:13)

If these truths make sense to you and you would like to receive Jesus right now as your personal Lord and Savior, a suggested prayer is provided below. The words you say are not as important as the attitude of your heart. If you truly want to place your faith in Jesus as your Savior and begin following Him as your Lord, God knows your heart and will answer your prayer.

A Prayer to Receive Jesus

"Dear Jesus, I know I have sinned and need your forgiveness. I believe you died for my sins and rose again. Please forgive me of my sins and help me live for you from this day forward. I trust in you now as my Savior, and I will follow you daily as my Lord. Thank you for saving me. Amen."

If you just prayed this prayer and meant it in your heart, at this very moment you can be certain that God has forgiven your sins and that you now have a home in Heaven.

To begin growing in your faith and learning how God wants you to live each day, there are several things you should start doing right away.

1. Attend a Bible-believing church on a regular basis.
2. Read the Bible each day, and study the Bible with other Christians.
3. Talk to God daily about your needs and concerns.
4. Tell other people about your decision to follow Christ.

The person who gave you this book may be willing to help you as you get started in your new journey of faith.

If this book has been a blessing to you, please share it with someone else who is interested in knowing more about Jesus. Before you know it, you will be telling other people why you believe in Jesus!

When you receive Jesus as your personal Savior and begin to read His Word, you find out that it is a living and powerful book. You learn things about God that you never knew before. You also learn things about yourself. You learn how to live for God. You learn how to build relationships with others that are healthy and loving. You learn how to forgive others when they hurt you. You learn how to overcome temptation and break bad habits. You learn how to get through the tough times in your life. I honestly do not know how people manage in this world without the Lord in their lives. I am so glad I decided to believe in Him. He has never let me down.

About the Author

Dr. Peter C. Hamilton has served as pastor of the First Baptist Church of Marysville, Ohio, since 2006. He teaches Bible and religion courses online for Liberty Baptist Theological Seminary in Lynchburg, VA, and James Sprunt Community College in Kenansville, NC. He has been married to his wife, Joyce, since 1981. They have two children and four grandchildren.

www.ingramcontent.com/pod-product-compliance
Lightning Source LLC
Chambersburg PA
CBHW031439040426
42444CB00006B/883